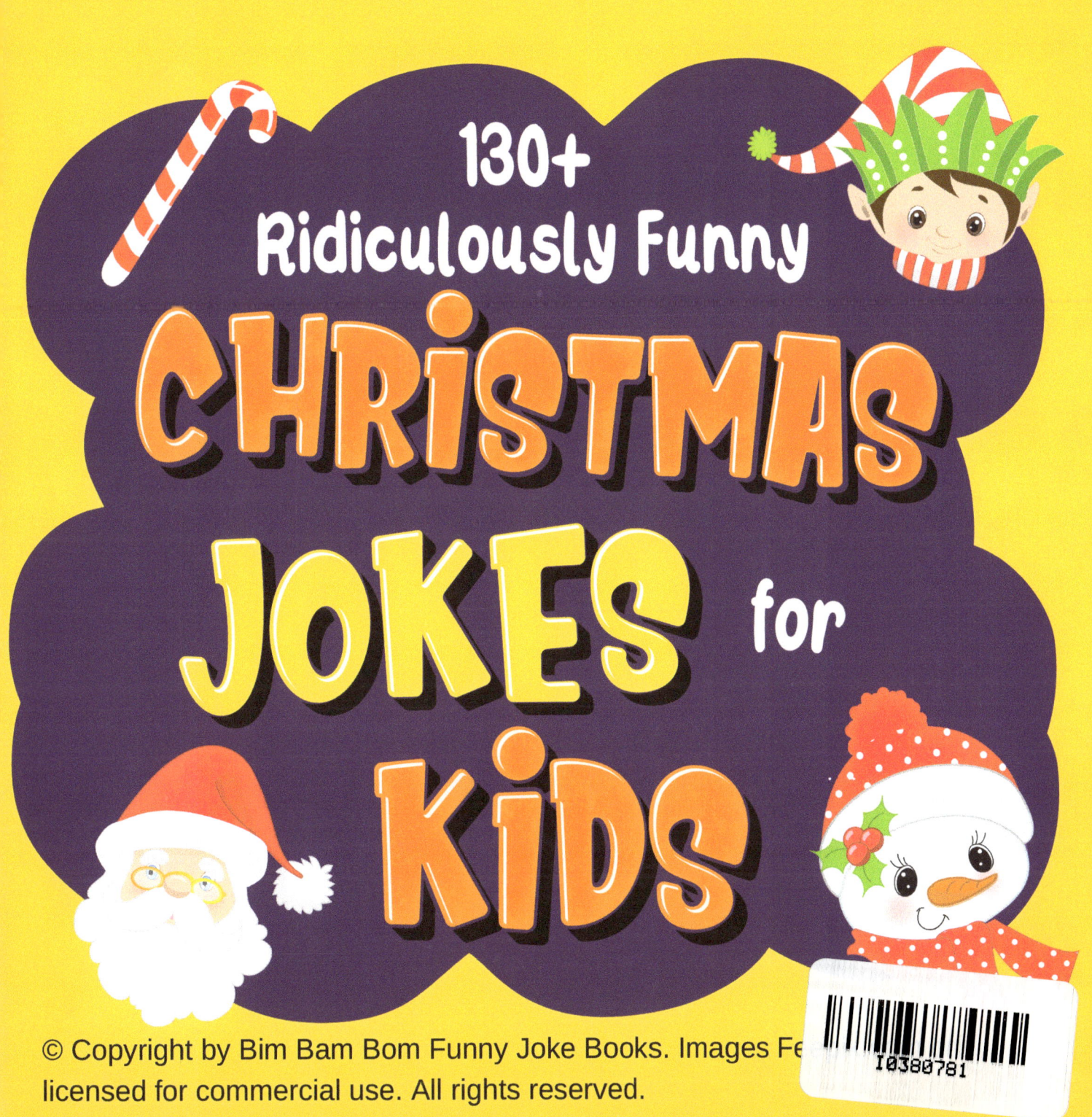

"Mom, can I please ask Santa for a new stuffed animal this Christmas?", Sally asks. "But sweetie," her mom replies, "You already have 3 amazing stuffed animals, why would you want another one?" Sally says, "Mom, why are you having a new baby while I'm still amazing?"

It's September when Santa walks up to an elf, who's at work in Santa's workshop. "Elf, we need to talk. You're slow at wrapping gifts. You're slow at feeding the reindeer. You're slow at cleaning the shop. Isn't there anything you can do quickly?" The elf replies, "Yes, Santa. I get tired quickly!"

Q: What is Santa's favorite TV quiz show?
A: Quizmas

Johnny, a young elf, comes home from school. "Dad, dad, I learned how to write today!", he says. "That's wonderful, Johnny," his dad replies, "And what did you write?" "I don't know," Johnny says, "I haven't learned how to read yet..."

Even though Santa lives on the North Pole, he still catches a cold sometimes. One morning, he wakes up sneezing and coughing. So, he walks into the pharmacy and says, "Do you have something against coughing?" The pharmacist replies, "Not at all, please go ahead!"

Q: How does a snowman get to work?
A: By icicle!

Knock, Knock.
Who's there?
Lettuce. Lettuce who?
Lettuce in. I've got your Christmas presents and it's freezing outside!

A young elf came home from school, with a black eye. "What happened?", Santa asked "I had a big fight with my classmate," the elf replied, "He called me a sissy." "And, what did you do?", Santa asked. The little elf said, "I hit him with my purse!"

Q: What's the favorite Christmas music of elves?
A: "Wrap" music!

A woman woke up in the morning, next to her husband. She rolled over and told him, "You know what I just dreamed? Santa would give me a pair of golden earrings! What do you think that means?" "Well baby," her husband replied, "Tonight you will know because it's Christmas Eve." That evening, the woman found a small gift-wrapped package underneath the Christmas tree. Delighted, she opened it, to find a book entitled "Dreams: What Do They Mean?"

Q: Where does Santa go to dance the Waltz?
A: The Snowball!

Q: Who is never hungry at Christmas?
A: The turkey: he's always stuffed!

Santa walks into his workshop for a motivational meeting with the elves: "Is there anyone in this group who thinks he's stupid? If so, please stand up!" Everybody remains seated. Santa: "Come on, surely there are some stupid elves here!" Then, one elf stands up. Santa: "Oh, Mary, do you think you're stupid?" Mary: "No, Santa. I just feel bad that you're the only one standing..."

Q: What do you call the sounds of people clapping their hands at Christmas?
A: Santapplause!

Q: It's white and it's flying upwards. What is it?
A: A crazy snowflake!

Santa and an elf are enjoying some time off in the summer. They decided to explore unknown territory and go for a walk across the desert. "Why did you bring that car door, elf?", Santa asks. "Santa," the elf replies, "I've got a good reason for that. When it gets too hot, I can open the window!"

Santa walks into the post office and asks for a $0.55 stamp. As the clerk hands him one, Santa says: "Can you please remove the price tag? It's a present..."

A man asks his wife what she would like to have for Christmas. "A divorce," she says. "I was hoping for something cheaper!", the man replies.

Q: Cross a Christmas tree with an apple and you get...?
A: A pineapple!

Q: What's the best thing to put into a Christmas Cake?
A: Your teeth!

Two snowmen are standing in a field. One snowman turned to the other and said "Do you smell carrots, too?"

Q: What does a snowman eat for breakfast?
A: Snowflakes!

Q: Who is Santa's favorite female pop singer?
A: Beyon-sleigh!

Q: What did Santa's wife say to Santa when she looked up at the sky?
A: Looks like rain, dear!

Q: Why does Santa have to import water to the North Pole?
A: Because there is no well!

On her Christmas wish list, a woman had asked for something that goes from 0-100 in less than 2 seconds. On Christmas Eve, her present was much smaller than she had expected. When she opened it, it was a scale...

Q: What do you call a kid that is afraid of Santa?
A: Claustrophobic!

Q: What would you call an elf if he also lived on the South Pole?
A: Bi-Polar!

Q: What does a reindeer say before he tells a joke to an elf?
Q: This one will 'sleigh' you!

Q: Why is Scrooge very fond of all of the reindeer?
A: Because every buck is close to his heart!

Q: What is the most popular food item on the menu in Santa's workshop cafeteria?
A: Icebergers!

Q: Why did Santa get a parking ticket while he was shopping?
A: He had left his sleigh in a snow parking zone!

A man is accused of theft and brought to trial. The judge asks, "How did you get all these Christmas presents?" The man replies: "Well, your honor, I went shopping really early." "How early?", the judge asks. The man says, "One hour before the shop opened!"

A polar bear sits in a bar at the North Pole, sipping a whiskey. An elf walks up to him and says, "Wow, it's not often that I see a polar bear drinking whiskey here!" To which the polar bear replies: "Yeah, but that's hardly a surprise at these prices."

Q: You find me in December, but not in any other month...
A: The letter D!

Q: Can an elf jump higher than the Washington Monument?
A: Of course! A monument can't jump, silly.

Q: If an elf has 14 presents in one hand and 6 Christmas trees in the other, what does he have?
A: Big hands!

Two elves are sitting on opposite sides of a river. One elf yells to the other: "How do I get to the other side of the river?" The second elf replies: "You ARE on the other side!"

Santa is reading the newspaper when his wife walks in and slams him on the head with a skillet. "Hey, what the snow are you doing?!", Santa yells. "I found a note in your suit, it says Rachel. You must be cheating on me!", Santa's wife says. Santa replies, "Sweetie, you know I've been thinking about getting a few extra reindeer to fly around the world for Christmas. Rachel is the name of the reindeer I went to take a look at last week."

Embarrassed, Santa's wife apologizes. However, a few weeks later, Santa gets hit on the head again. He turns around and sees his wife with a skillet in her hand. "What is it this time?!", Santa says, angrily. His wife replies: "There's a phone call for you: It's your reindeer…"

Q: Why is it a bad idea to write a list with a broken pencil?
A: Because it is pointless!

Q: How does a Christmas angel greet another angel?
A: "Halo!"

Q: What do sheep say to each other at Christmas?
A: "Season's bleatings!"

Q: How is the alphabet different on Christmas Day?
A: There's Noel!

Q: What is the best place to find reindeer?
A: Where you left them!

Q: How do you lift a frozen car?
A: With a Jack Frost!

Q: What is as light as a feather yet as big as Santa Claus?
A: Santa's shadow!

Q: What are Santa Claus's favorite potato chips?
A: Crisp Pringles!

Q: What falls at the North Pole but never gets hurt?
A: Snow!

Q: How did Scrooge win the basketball game?
A: The ghost of Christmas passed!

Santa takes Rudolph the red-nosed reindeer to the vet because he is cross-eyed. The vet says: "Let's have a look," and picks up Rudolph to examine his eyes. After looking at his eyes for a while, the vet says: "I'm going to have to put him down." "Wait, what?", Santa replies, "Just because he is cross-eyed?" Vet: "No, because he is really heavy!"

Q: What does Santa say when he arrives back on the North Pole, after delivering presents all around the world?
A: Ho-ho-home sweet home!

Q: What do elves say when Santa is taking attendance at his workshop?
A: Present!

A policeman stops an old man driving a car. The man has a white beard and wears a red suit. As the policeman approaches the car, he notices a reindeer in the front seat. "What are you doing with that reindeer?", he asked, "You should take it to the zoo!" The next week, the police officer sees the same old man with the reindeer again in the front seat. This time, both are wearing sunglasses. The policeman pulls the car over. "I thought you were going to take it to the zoo!" The old man replied, "I did. We had such a great time, Rudolph and I are going to the beach this weekend!"

Q: What do you call a snowman with a six pack?
A: An abdominal snowman!

Q: What do you call a frozen elf hanging from the ceiling?
A: An elfcicle!

Q: Why was the snowman searching through a bag of carrots?
A: He was picking his nose!

Q: What did the Christmas tree say to the ornament?
A: Quit hanging around!

Q: What did Adam say to his wife, the day before Christmas?
A: It's Christmas, Eve!

Q: What are the best Christmas shirts made from?
A: Fleece Navidad!

It's early spring when an elf walks into a job center in San Francisco. "Wow, a talking elf," says the clerk. "With your talent, I'm sure we can find you a gig in the circus." "The circus?", says the elf, "What does a circus want with a gift wrapper?"

Q: Why are Christmas trees so fond of the past?
A: Because the present's beneath them!

Q: Why did the Christmas tree go to the barber?
A: It needed to be trimmed!

Q: What is Santa's favorite motorbike?
A: A Holly Davidson!

One day, an arctic fox walks into Santa's workshop and asks an elf if they sell apples. The elf says, "No, we don't sell apples." The arctic fox goes home and returns the next day, "Hello, do you sell apples?" Again, the elf says they don't. The fox leaves the workshop but returns the very next day.

"There he is again," says the elf to himself. And sure enough, the arctic fox asks the elf if they sell apples. This time though, the elf is so fed up with this stupid fox that he says, "No, fox, we don't sell apples! Or pears, or oranges, or bananas. This is the North Pole! If you come back one more time and ask me for apples, I will nail your paws to the floor!" The arctic fox leaves quickly.

But...the elf can't believe his eyes when he sees the arctic fox walk through the door again, the next day. This time, the arctic fox asks, "Do you have any nails?" The elf says, "No, we don't have any nails." "Okay, good," the arctic fox says, "Do you sell apples?"

One day, an elf went to Santa's house and found Santa playing chess with a penguin in the living room. Astonished, the elf watched the game for a couple of minutes. "I can't believe my eyes!" he exclaimed. "That is the smartest penguin I have ever seen." To which Santa replied: "Mwoah, he's not that smart. I've beaten him three games out of five!"

Santa and his wife were going to see a movie and ordered a taxi. As they left the house, their cat ran back in. Santa went back inside because they didn't want the cat to be shut in the house while they were away. Meanwhile, Santa's wife stepped into the taxi. Because she didn't want the taxi driver to know that Santa's house was empty, she told him that Santa had just gone inside to say goodbye to her mother. A short while later, Santa also stepped into the cab and said: "My apologies for taking so long, but that stupid old thing was hiding under the bed. I had to poke her with a broomstick to get her to come out!"

Q: What do snowmen call their offspring?
A: Chill-dren!

On his Christmas wish list, a man has written an unusual request: "I live in New York, but my sister lives in France. I never liked flying that much. Santa, could you please make a highway from New York to Paris?" So Santa sends the man an e-mail. "I love to grant your wishes, but you're asking for too much here. Building that bridge would require 80% of my elves working on it for more than a year! Isn't there something else you would rather like for Christmas?

The man replies, "You're right, Santa, let me change my wish then. I have had a lot of bad luck dating girls. Can you help me find a girl to date?" One day later, Santa replies, "So, that highway: do you want that with two lanes or four lanes?"

Q: Why did Santa hire elves to work in his workshop?
A: Because the seven dwarfs were too busy!

Q. What is Santa Claus's favorite measurement in the metric system?
A. The Santameter!

Q: What did Santa say when the elf ate the entire cake?
A: "You're so elfish!"

Q: What do you call Santa when he stops a Netflix show halfway through, to get some drinks from the kitchen?
A: Santa pause!

Q: What would Santa be called if he was from the South of the U.S.?
A: Louisiana Claus!

Q: Where does Santa sleep when he is on vacation?
A: At a Ho-ho-ho-tel!

An elf sits down in the cafeteria in Santa's workshop. All of a sudden, an elephant walks in, buys a donut and leaves. The elf is astounded, "Wow, that's so strange!" To which the elf behind the counter says, "Yeah, I agree, up until today he always ordered a chocolate chip cookie..."

Q: What is a librarian's favorite Christmas song?
A: Silent Night!

Santa is having dinner with 5 elves. Santa says: "I just had this tablecloth cleaned, so don't spill any soup on it. If you do, I will deduct $1 from your salary for each stain." Then, Santa gets up to get some more bread. When he returns, he sees that one of the elves has spilled soup on the tablecloth and he's using his spoon to make the stain even bigger. "What do you think you're doing?!", Santa yells. The elf replies, "I'm turning 3 stains into one, Santa, so I only lose $1..."

Q: Who is a Christmas tree's favorite singer?
A: Spruce Springsteen!

Q: How did the ornament get addicted to Christmas?
A: He was hooked on trees his whole life!

Q: Why did Santa Claus cry when he watched 'The Lion King'?
A: He felt santamental!

Q: Why does Santa go down the chimney?
A: Because it soots him!

Q: It's red and says "Oh Oh Oh". What is it?
A: Santa walking backwards!

Q: Who was Santa's first love?
A: Mary Christmas!

It's 2 days before Christmas when a man calls his daughter in New-Zealand. He says: "I'm afraid I've got some bad news: your mom and I are getting a divorce on Christmas day. These last 40 years were great, but we've decided to go our own way from now on."

The daughter is in shock. After a few seconds, she gets a grip of herself and says: "Dad, you can't do this! Last week everything was fine! This is so sudden…this ain't right….I'm sure my brother John in France agrees. Have you already spoken to him?". Her dad replies, "No, I haven't, I called you first." "OK," his daughter responds, "Here's what we're going to do."

"I'll call John in the morning. John and I will jump on the first plane home to discuss this stupid divorce idea with you two." The father agrees and hangs up the phone. He walks into the living room and says to his wife: "It worked! The kids are coming over for Christmas and they're even paying for their own flight tickets!"

Two blondes are in a shopping mall to do their Christmas shopping. They decide to play a game. One blonde says to the other: "If you can guess how many candies I have in my pocket, you can have all four of them."

Q: What is the favorite movie of Santa's cat?
A: The Sound of Mewsic.

Q: What do you call Santa after he filed for bankruptcy?
A: Saint Nickel-less!

Q: How can you tell Santa is a jiu jitsu expert?
A: He has a black belt!

Q: What language do Santa Claus and the elves speak?
A: North Polish!

Q: Why did Santa Claus put a watch on his sleigh?
A: Because he wanted to see time fly!

Q: Where do you find chilli beans?
A: At the north pole!

Q: What do you call an elf who just has won a million dollars?
A: Welfy!

Q: Why did the elf go see a psychologist?
A: Because he had low elf esteem!

Q: What name did Santa give his dog?
A: Santa Paws!

Q: Why didn't the skeleton go to the Christmas party?
A: He had no-body to go with!

Q: What did the beaver say to the Christmas Tree?
A: Nice gnawing you!

Q: Who is the favorite artist of Santa's wife?
A: Elf-is Presley!

Q: What is a skunk's favorite Christmas song?
A: Jingle smells!

Q: What is the first thing elves learn at school?
A: The elf-abet!

Knock knock.
Who's there?
Snow.
Snow who?
Snow business like show business!

Q: What is an elf's favorite car to drive?
A: A toy-Yoda!

Q: Who delivers presents to the fish in the ocean?
A: Santa Jaws!

Q: Which state does Santa visit first on Christmas Eve?
A: Idaho-ho-ho!

Q: What do elves post on Instagram when Santa isn't looking?
A: Elfies!

Q: Did Rudolph the red-nosed reindeer go to school?
A: No. He was elf-taught!

Q: How do you know a family doesn't celebrate Christmas?
A: The lights are on in their house, but nobody's a gnome!

Q: Where does Santa go when he's feeling ill?
A: To the elf center!

Q: Why did the turkey join Santa's Christmas party band?
A: Because it had the drumsticks!

Q: Why do cats take forever to wrap their presents?
A: They want them to be purr-fect!

Q: What do dolphins sing at Christmas?
A: Christmas Corals!

Santa and an elf are delivering presents on Christmas Eve. They're trying to be quiet, they don't want to wake up any children. But then Santa steps on a tree branch. A man opens the window and asks: "Who's there?". Santa says, "Meow!" "Ah, I see," the man says, "It's just a cat." Then, the elf also steps on the same tree branch. As Santa looks at him angrily, the window opens again. The same man, now somewhat suspicious, asks, "Hello, who is there?" To which the elf replies, "Nobody, it's just the cat again!"

Q: What did the cat say when she saw that only one of the fifty presents under the Christmas tree had her name on it?
A: You've got to be kitten me.

One morning, Santa's favorite reindeer has fallen ill, so he has the elves fly in a vet. As the vet examines the reindeer in the stables, Santa is waiting outside. After a while, the vet walks outside and asks Santa for a screwdriver. Santa hands him one. The vet goes back inside, leaving Santa behind, feeling anxious.

A few minutes later, the vet comes outside again. This time, he asks for a hammer and a chisel. Santa gives him what he asks for, but he's starting to feel really nervous now.

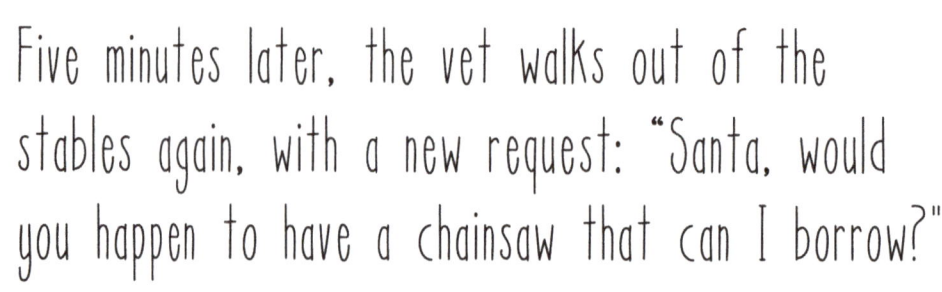

Five minutes later, the vet walks out of the stables again, with a new request: "Santa, would you happen to have a chainsaw that can I borrow?"

Santa is shocked and asks the vet: "Is the reindeer going to be OK?". "I can't tell yet," the vet replies, "I haven't been able to open my toolkit yet…"

Q: Why do Santa's reindeer stop running every 20 seconds?
A: Because Santa keeps saying "Ho Ho Ho!"

Santa: "Why do reindeer wear orange nail polish?" Elf: "I don't have a clue." Santa: "To hide in Christmas trees." Elf: "Come on, Santa, I have never seen a reindeer in a Christmas tree." Santa: "See, it works!"

Q: What did the little candle say to the big candle?
A: I'm going out tonight!

Bernard the elf enters Santa's reindeer stables and asks the elf in charge, "Can I please borrow a reindeer for a while?" The other elf replies, "Sure, Bernard, how long?" "I'd like the longest one you have,", Bernard says, "we're with 6 elves!"

It's an ordinary day at Santa's workshop when one of the elves farts loudly. As the smell starts to spread, Santa Claus turns to him and says: "How dare you fart in front of me!" The elf replies: "I'm terribly sorry, Santa, I didn't realize it was your turn!"

Q: What do you get if you cross a tiger with a snowman?
A: Frostbite!

In a shopping mall, a girl walks up to Santa and sits on his lap. Santa asks her, "Hello little girl, what's your name?" The girl doesn't say anything and gives Santa an angry look. Santa asks her once again for her name. Finally, the girl says: "I told you my name this morning, at school. Do you mean to say that you ALREADY forgot it?!"

Q: What did the peanut butter say to the strawberry at Christmas?
A: "'Tis the season to be jelly!"

Q: What do elves sing at an elf's birthday party?
A: Freeze a jolly good fellow!

During the annual North Pole fair, Santa decides to visit a fortune-teller. He enters the tent and asks the woman how much she charges. "Two questions for $100," she says. "Wow...isn't that super expensive?", Santa asks. "Yes, it is," the fortune-teller replies, "And what is your second question?"

Q: Why do reindeer make terrible dance partners?
A: They've got two left feet!

Q: What is even more amazing than a talking polar bear?
A: A spelling bee!

Q: Which of Santa's reindeer has the worst manners?
A: RUDE-olph!